MY LIFE AS A JEW

- **Trevor Guy**
- **Sue Mizon**
- **Paul Morgan**

DREF WEN

The Shema

*Hear, O Israel: The Lord our God is one; and you shall love
the Lord your God with all your heart and with all your
soul and with all your strength. These words which
I command you this day shall be upon your heart.
You shall teach them carefully to your children and shall
talk about them when you are in your house and when you
walk by the way and when you lie down and when you rise.
You shall bind them as a sign on your hand and they shall
be as frontlets between your eyes and you shall write them
on the doorposts of your house and on your gates.*

Special Photography Pat and Charles Aithie (ffotograff)

Design Michael Leaman Design Partnership

The books in this series are also available in Welsh-language editions.

Photographs Trevor Guy (ESIS) front cover centre right, pages 6 centre, 21 foot, 28 foot left and right,
30 top and centre; Magnum page 15 foot; Paul Morgan (ESIS) page 31; Jill Ranford (ffotograff) page 23 right.
All other photographs are by Pat and Charles Aithie (ffotograff). Some of these (often indicated by corner mountings) are
reproduced from photographs kindly provided by the families concerned. *Artwork* Netzer Olami pages 14, 15;
Tessa John page 17. *Map* Julian Baker Illustrations page 6. We have made every effort to contact owners of
copyright material and apologise if in any instance we have been unsuccessful.

Contents

My community

Ben: I like playing on my computer and listening to music on the stereo but I don't have a favourite band.

BEN Benjamin Joel Soffa is my full name but my family and friends just call me Ben. I go to a school near the city centre in Cardiff.

My family are **Jews**. We go to the Cardiff New **Synagogue**. Not all Jews follow their faith in the same way. At our synagogue, we are called **Reform** Jews. People in school know I'm Jewish because I have time off for the big festivals.

Our synagogue is two miles from our house. It used to be a Christian chapel. I see other Jewish people from my community about twice a week. That's when we go to worship on Friday and Saturday. There's a youth group which meets about once a month. Sometimes we go to places together, like Techniquest, the science discovery centre.

Ben: I enjoy celebrating the festivals with my family. You can see us in this photograph. I've got a sister, Vicky, who is nine.

SARAH My name is Sarah Lyons and I live with my parents, Alan and Laura. My younger brother, Joshua, and my sister, Malka, are twins. We are an **Orthodox** Jewish family. We live on the west side of Cardiff. There used to be two Orthodox synagogues in Cardiff but the one near our house closed down. Now, we use a house nearby for prayer. We have to travel further to meet our other Jewish friends. My best friends at the other synagogue are Natasha, Natalie and Amber. We go to Jewish Lads and Girls Brigade together.

THINK ABOUT:

Are all Jewish communities the same? How do they differ?

Ben and Sarah belong to a number of different communities. How many can you identify?

What sorts of things do Ben and Sarah do because they belong to Jewish communities?

Sarah: I like being on my own but also with my friends. On Tuesdays, I go to a club called Jewish Lads and Girls Brigade.

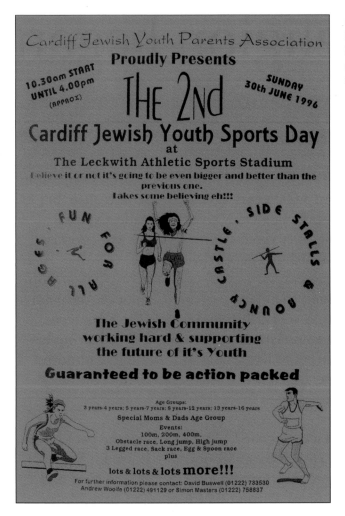

Ben: It's good to do things together as a community.

BEN Belonging to the Jewish community means that there is always someone you can go to for help. You can always walk into a synagogue and be accepted. So, if you visit another town, you will always find new friends in the Jewish community. You get a feeling of belonging wherever you go.

THINGS TO DO

Think of some of the communities to which you belong. Using a blank sheet of paper put yourself in the centre and map these communities around yourself.

Ben and Sarah have told us about themselves. Write a few paragraphs about yourself in the same way. You can include any information about yourself you think is important. Add a photograph or a self-portrait if you like.

Ben and Sarah do lots of things their school friends don't do. Write out the sort of conversation that one of them might have with a friend. Imagine how Ben or Sarah might explain how much they enjoy being part of a Jewish community.

Where my religion began

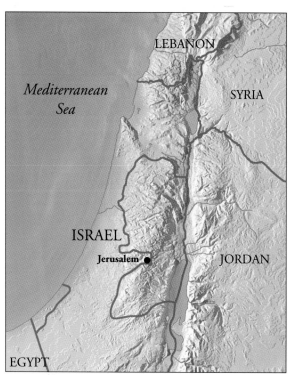

Israel and its neighbours today

BEN **Israel** is a very special place for Jews because of its history. It's a place where most of the people are Jews.

The very first Jew was a **nomad** called Abraham, who lived about 4,000 years ago. He came to realise that there was only one God; and God made a special agreement, or covenant, with him. He was promised a land in which his people would live.

In time Isaac, then Jacob, became leader of Abraham's family. Jacob was also called Israel. The Jews were given the name Israelites because of him. During his life, they went to live in Egypt. After a few hundred years there, they grew into a small nation; but they also became slaves.

God used a man called Moses to bring the people out of Egypt. He led them around the desert for forty years before they arrived back in the land God had promised them. During that time, God gave Moses laws on **Mount Sinai**.

*Sarah: My mam has tried to talk Joshua into going to Israel for his **bar mitzvah** but he isn't keen. He's afraid there may be a war.*

THINK ABOUT:

Why has there been fighting in Israel since 1948?

Why do many Jews feel so strongly that they have a right to the land of Israel?

When two groups of people believe strongly that they are both right, how can they find a solution?

Ben: My dad had this book as a child. The picture shows Moses being found as a baby by the Egyptian princess.

Years later, King David chose **Jerusalem** as his capital city. His son Solomon built a temple there. You can still see part of a wall of a later temple in Jerusalem today. It is a very holy place for us.

Over the years Israel was often invaded. Many Jews were forced to leave their land. In the end, there wasn't really a country you could call Israel any more.

After the Second World War the Jews were allowed to set up their own state of Israel again. Jews from many different countries went back. Unfortunately, the Arabs saw Israel as *their* home, and this has caused problems ever since.

One day I would like to go to Israel, but I would not want to live there. If I did, I would have to go into the army because of the problems there. I don't think I would like that.

Ben: *The Western Wall is all that remains of the temple in Jerusalem which the Romans destroyed.*

THINGS TO DO

Draw a map of Israel and mark Jerusalem on it. Write a sentence underneath to say why Jerusalem is so special to Jews.

Draw a picture postcard from Israel. You might like to use some of the photographs in this book for ideas for the front of your card. Imagine you are sending it home to a friend while you are on holiday. What would be the most interesting facts about Israel you could tell your friend in three short sentences?

Is there a place which means something special to you? Describe it and explain why it is important.

Starting out in life

> God said to Abraham...
> every male among you
> shall be circumcised.
> And you shall be
> circumcised in the flesh
> of your foreskin;
> and it shall be a sign of
> the covenant between
> me and you.
>
> Genesis chapter 17 verses 9 to 11.

Sarah: Abraham and his son were the first to be circumcised as Jews.

SARAH'S MAM We have a ceremony called **brit milah** for baby boys. We remove the little bit of skin that covers the end of their penis. This operation is called circumcision. It's done when the baby is eight days old. Sometimes non-Jewish boys have to be circumcised because their foreskin is causing a problem. That's not why Jewish boys have it done. It is a very private part of the body but, for men, it's an important aspect of being Jews.

The thing I remember most about Joshua being circumcised is what happened when it was all over. I was upstairs feeding him, because it was the only way to stop him crying. Malka, his twin sister, caught hold of his hand while I was feeding him. It was the only time she ever did that, as if she were trying to comfort him.

SARAH I was very young when Joshua had his brit milah so I don't remember a lot about it. Mam says that Grampa held Joshua so that **Rabbi** Book could do the circumcision. It's really important for Jews. All our family were there, and friends and

THINK ABOUT:

What kinds of thoughts and feelings do you think Joshua's mother had at his brit milah?

Why do you think it was almost like a party after Joshua's brit milah?

What do you think Sarah meant when she said that circumcision was a sign of the covenant that God had made with Abraham?

Sarah: Here I am with Joshua and Malka.

Sarah: Here are Joshua and Malka the day after they were born. Grandma is holding Joshua on the left and Mam has Malka on the right.

FACT FILE

Brit milah The name for the ceremony of circumcision. The name means covenant of circumcision. Circumcision doesn't make a boy a Jew but the ceremony shows that the parents are going to bring their child up as a Jew.

Rabbi A leader of a Jewish community who helps people in many ways. The word rabbi means teacher. Teaching about the Jewish faith is the most important part of a rabbi's job.

Covenant A promise or agreement. Jews believe that God made an agreement with them. He would take care of them because he had chosen them to be his special people.

Cheder This is a school held in the synagogue. It is sometimes called Religion School. There are classes in the evenings or on Sundays, to teach Jewish children about their religion.

people who wanted to share the occasion with us. When it had been done, a drop of wine was put on the baby's lips and he was given his name. It was almost like a party afterwards.

I know circumcision is important because it's a way of making a **covenant** with God. Joshua says he's learnt a bit about it in **Cheder**. We do it because God told Abraham to circumcise all the males in his family. God said it would be a sign that God had made a covenant with Abraham.

THINGS TO DO

If you had a younger brother who was going to have his brit milah, who would you like to be there? Make a list of the people you would invite to your house.

Imagine that you are Joshua's brother or sister and have been at his brit milah. Write a letter to a friend or relative about what happened.

Can you remember a baby being born? Were there any celebrations? Was there a ceremony? Write a paragraph about anything that you know happened after a baby had been born. If you can't write about a real birth, make up a story yourself.

Following the path

Hebrew text at top of Ark: השתחוו ליהוה בהדרת־קדש

BEN At the front of our synagogue there is a cupboard with curtains across the front. We call it the **Ark**. Our holy books are kept in it, written on scrolls. Each one of them costs thousands of pounds. That is because they have to be written by hand in the Hebrew language. It takes months to write one.

SARAH'S MAM All the scrolls are important, but the most important one is called the **Torah**. We believe the Torah was given by God to Moses.

Every **Shabbat**, somebody reads a section from the Torah. It is a great honour to do the reading. Usually the rabbi does it; but sometimes somebody else will read a piece, after practising hard. The reader follows the words with a special pointer called a yad. We don't touch the scroll with our fingers, both as a sign of respect and to keep it clean.

Sometimes people say our Torah is the same as the Old Testament in the Christian Bible, but that is not quite right. The Torah is part of a bigger book called the **Tenakh**. It's the Tenakh that is the same as the Old Testament.

Ben: Each scroll has a special cover and is decorated with a breastplate and bells. You can tell how important they are just by looking at them.

THINK ABOUT:

How do Jews show how important the Torah is?

Is there somebody special that you look up to and go to for advice?

How important do you think it is to keep the Law?

Sarah: When the Chief Rabbi for Britain visited our synagogue, he joined in our lessons and helped my sister with her Hebrew.

Ben: Yad means hand. It is usually shaped like a hand with a pointing finger.

SARAH The Torah is so important that, at one time, ordinary people weren't allowed to read it. They would be told what it said by the rabbi.

BEN Rabbi Elaina is very important because she's the religious leader in our community. People respect her because you can always talk to her. It's not just because she has "Rabbi" in front of her name. It's who she is, the sort of person she is.

Ben: People turn to Rabbi Elaina for advice.

THINGS TO DO

The Jewish holy books are written in Hebrew. Hebrew is a very ancient language which is written from right to left. In the Torah, it is written without vowels. Copy some Hebrew writing from the picture of the Shema on page 12.

Ben talks about Rabbi Elaina being the kind of person you would look up to for leadership. Make a list of things that you think would make a person a good leader.

Think about your favourite book, or one that is special to you. Write a paragraph explaining why you like it, or what makes it special.

What we believe

Sarah: *Any Jewish person who comes to our house would kiss their hand then touch the mezuzah.*

SARAH On most of the door frames in our house there's a little box. It's called a mezuzah. Sometimes, I kiss it when I come into the room. That's because it's holy. There's a copy of the **Shema** in every one of them.

BEN I accept what it says in the Shema about God. It reminds us that there is only one God and we must worship only him. I think this goes back to the days when some people used to worship lots of gods. It was a big change for the first Jews to think there was only one God.

Probably, the most important thing we believe is that we have a covenant with God, that we are his chosen people. We are supposed to show other people a better way to be, even when others are being hateful.

Another thing that shows what we believe is keeping Shabbat. Dad says we do this because it is a direct commandment. It reminds us that God is the creator of everything and all things belong to him. In the very old days, before workers had holidays, we were the only people who gave their workers and animals a day off every week. They had Shabbat off as well as the bosses. We have always done this because it shows we respect human life and know that rest is important.

THINK ABOUT:

Why do Jews keep one day of the week special and different from the rest?

Is it good to be chosen for something? What is it like not be chosen? How do you think Jews feel about being God's chosen people?

How can you show people a better way to behave when they are being hateful to you?

שְׁמַע יִשְׂרָאֵל יְדֹוָה אֱלֹדֵינוּ יְדֹוָה אֶחָד וְאָהַבְתָּ אֵת
יְדֹוָה אֱלֹדֶיךָ בְּכָל לְבָבְךָ וּבְכָל נַפְשְׁךָ וּבְכָל מְאֹדֶךָ וְהָיוּ
הַדְּבָרִים הָאֵלֶּה אֲשֶׁר אָנֹכִי מְצַוְּךָ הַיּוֹם עַל לְבָבֶךָ וְשִׁנַּנְתָּם
לְבָנֶיךָ וְדִבַּרְתָּ בָּם בְּשִׁבְתְּךָ בְּבֵיתֶךָ וּבְלֶכְתְּךָ בַדֶּרֶךְ
וּבְשָׁכְבְּךָ וּבְקוּמֶךָ וּקְשַׁרְתָּם לְאוֹת עַל יָדֶךָ וְהָיוּ לְטֹטָפֹת
בֵּין עֵינֶיךָ וּכְתַבְתָּם עַל מְזֻזוֹת בֵּיתֶךָ וּבִשְׁעָרֶיךָ
וְהָיָה אִם שָׁמֹעַ תִּשְׁמְעוּ אֶל מִצְוֹתַי אֲשֶׁר אָנֹכִי
מְצַוֶּה אֶתְכֶם הַיּוֹם לְאַהֲבָה אֶת יְדֹוָה אֱלֹדֵיכֶם וּלְעָבְדוֹ
בְּכָל לְבַבְכֶם וּבְכָל נַפְשְׁכֶם וְנָתַתִּי מְטַר אַרְצְכֶם בְּעִתּוֹ
יוֹרֶה וּמַלְקוֹשׁ וְאָסַפְתָּ דְגָנֶךָ וְתִירֹשְׁךָ וְיִצְהָרֶךָ וְנָתַתִּי
עֵשֶׂב בְּשָׂדְךָ לִבְהֶמְתֶּךָ וְאָכַלְתָּ וְשָׂבָעְתָּ הִשָּׁמְרוּ לָכֶם
פֶּן יִפְתֶּה לְבַבְכֶם וְסַרְתֶּם וַעֲבַדְתֶּם אֱלֹדִים אֲחֵרִים

Sarah: *This is what the Shema looks like in Hebrew. You can see it in English on the second page of this book.*

SARAH We believe God is everywhere. He's eternal and he's here, there and everywhere. We also believe that at some time the **Messiah** is going to come.

Sarah: *No-one can see God but we believe he created the world. Before the world was made, there was nothing except God.*

THINGS TO DO

The Shema tells us the most important thing that Jews believe. In one sentence, write on a piece of paper the most important thing that you believe. Make and decorate a small box or container in which you can keep your paper.

Look at the Ten Commandments in the Bible. You can find them in the book of Exodus Chapter 20. Write down what the first four say about God.

Read carefully through what Ben and Sarah say in this chapter. Look for four things that Jews believe about God. Make a poster showing the four beliefs that you find.

FACT FILE

Shema A passage in Deuteronomy which is very important to Jews. In Hebrew, it begins with the word "Shema" which means "Hear!" The Shema says that God is the only God and must be loved and obeyed.

Messiah A special person who many Jews believe is coming to put an end to all evil. He will bring in a new age of peace and friendship between all people.

Right and wrong

Ben: *These are the Ten Commandments written in Hebrew on the board in our synagogue.*

BEN There are lots of things we have to do because we are Jews. Many of these rules are just commonsense. No-one would really disagree with them. We mustn't kill people. We mustn't steal. We must respect our fathers and mothers. It's not so obvious why we have to obey some of the others. I don't know why we can only eat certain sorts of food. We just do it because God tells us in the Torah.

I follow what the Torah says because I think it is right. I obey the laws just because I agree with them and believe in them, not because I'll get any final reward.

The teaching in the Torah isn't only about religious things. It covers every aspect of life. The Ten Commandments are the central rules; but I think all the **moral laws**, and some of the business laws, are important.

Everyone does things that are wrong, sometimes. I usually try to be good, but now and again I do wrong things because I just don't think. Rabbi Elaina told us the most important thing is accepting that you've done something wrong and saying sorry to the person who has been affected. If I have done something wrong that affects only God, I have to let God know that I am sorry for it. There is one special day in the year when we ask for forgiveness for all our **sins**. That is **Yom Kippur**. It is a very serious time when we think about our past and how we can be better in the future.

THINK ABOUT:

Ben says that everybody would agree with some laws. He gives some examples. Do you think he is right about them?

How do you feel when you do something you know is wrong?

What stops people doing wrong things?

Ben: *The cartoon figures on these pages are from a calendar. They remind us how to behave. To be a good Jew, I have to have good manners, be kind to other people and care for animals too.*

help an elderly person by cleaning their home

AUGUST		is	for			HELPING
1992						אב - אלול 5752 AV - ELUL 5752
Sun.	Mon.	Tues.	Wed.	Thurs.	Fri.	Sat.
						1 מסעי
2	3	4	5	6	7	8 דברים
9 Tisha B'Av	10	11	12	13	14	15 ואתחנן
16	17	18	19	20	21	22 עקב
23	24	25	26	27	28	29 ראה
30 אלול א	31					

*Tora Reading for the Diaspora on Aug. 1:מטות-מסעי

... offer to trade your time with an elderly person — you'll spend an hour cleaning if she/he spends an hour telling you stories about her/his life.
... get together a group of people who will take turns doing the shopping with (or for) someone who has difficulty doing it themselves.
... think of institutions (eg, for people with disabilities, the elderly, or the sick) in your area where people live cut off from normal life. Set time aside, with friends, to help some of them get out for a while — or think of creative ways to take the "outside" world in:

14

Doing Heshbon Nefesh (an accounting of the soul) on Yom Kippur

Ben: *At Yom Kippur, my calendar reminds me to think carefully about my life.*

SARAH Sometimes it's hard to keep all the rules. If you invite a friend around on Shabbat, there are some things you can't do – you mustn't write anything, for instance. You're not supposed to say God's name when you read it in the Torah. That's because God's name is so holy. Anything with God's name in it is holy. So if we drop a **Siddur**, we kiss it when we pick it up.

In Jerusalem, when people are upset by something bad which happens, they sometimes come to pray at the Western Wall.

FACT FILE

Moral laws Laws that are to do with what is good and bad behaviour.

Sins Things that are against God's law.

Yom Kippur This is Hebrew for the Day of Atonement. It is the day when Jews ask God to forgive them for all the bad things they have done in the year. Jews go without food and drink and spend the day worshipping God. Going without food and drink is called fasting.

Siddur The Jewish prayer book. In it are the words for all the services. You will find a picture of one on page 20.

THINGS TO DO

Do you think that there is one rule that is more important than any other? Design a poster to remind people of your "golden rule".

When people do bad things, others are often affected. Look carefully at the picture of the woman crying at the Western Wall of the Temple. What might have made her so upset? Write your own story to go with the picture.

Ben's calendar for September asks him to think carefully about his life. This is to prepare him for Yom Kippur. Write your own answers to the questions: "What do you plan to be like and to have done in one year's time? How are you going to achieve this?"

Daily life

SARAH My brother's got a red and white **kippah**. He was given it by a friend who supports Manchester United. Jewish men and boys wear a kippah for prayer and going to the synagogue. Some Orthodox women wear a hat or a wig all the time so no-one sees their hair except their husbands.

Men also wear a **tallit**. It reminds us that there are 613 different laws in the Torah. There are rules about everything we do – what we eat, what we wear, and how we behave towards other people.

BEN The Torah teaches us a lot about being a good person. I don't find the laws a problem. They never really stop me from doing anything I want to do.

Some Jewish people will try to keep all the rules. Some people only try to keep the ones they think are still important in today's world. As you can imagine, this leads to a lot of talk about what Jews should and shouldn't do.

SARAH There are food laws that say what Jews can and can't eat. You can only eat meat of animals that chew grass and have split hooves; and you can only eat fish with scales and fins. We have to make sure that any meat we eat has been prepared in a certain way by a special butcher. Food you can eat is called **kosher**. Food that's forbidden is called treyfah. We don't eat pork or anything that's made from a pig because it's treyfah.

Sarah: A tallit has blue or black stripes along the edges. It is the fringe with a special tassel at each corner which reminds us of the laws in the Torah.

THINK ABOUT:

Ben says that not all Jews have the same ideas about the rules that affect their daily lives. Why do you think this is?

Do laws ever stop you doing what you want to do? Is that a good or a bad thing?

Sarah gives an example of when it is all right to break the Shabbat laws. Can you think of other examples when it might be better to break laws than to keep them?

Ben: Until a few years ago, there used to be a kosher butcher in Cardiff, but now a van comes from Birmingham once a week.

Sarah: In our friends' kitchen, they use different colours to show what is for meat and what is for milk.

KOSHER

TREYFAH

Sarah: These are some of the animals that are kosher or treyfah.

Another law says we are not to mix meat and milk foods at the same meal. So many Jews have two sets of sinks, cookers and so on in their kitchens.

One of the most important laws is keeping Shabbat holy. On that day we're not supposed to sew, garden, cut flowers, write, cook, or touch money. We're not supposed to switch on the electricity; but we could if it would save someone's life.

THINGS TO DO

Draw your own tallit. Around it, write some laws that you think we all ought to keep.

Think about the sorts of animals and fish that Sarah says she can eat. Can you think of some that she can and some that she cannot? Work this out with a partner. Then write them out in two columns.

Write out menus for two meals. In one, make sure that any meat and fish is kosher and that you do not mix milk and meat. In the other, show the sort of meal that a Jew could not eat because it contains treyfah food and mixes milk and meat.

Kosher	Treyfah

FACT FILE

Kippah A head covering worn by boys and men as a sign of respect for God. Some are shown in the pictures on the opposite page.

Tallit A shawl worn while praying. See the picture on the opposite page.

Kosher Anything which Jews are allowed to eat or wear.

17

Growing up as a Jew

Ben: *I had my bar mitzvah nearly a year ago.*

BEN When you understand and are ready to accept the laws or commandments, a special service is held in the synagogue at which you become bar mitzvah. That means "son of the commandments". The idea is that you are meant to obey the laws as a child should obey a parent.

I had a long preparation for my bar mitzvah. I had to go to Cheder from around the age of six. Then, in the school year before my bar mitzvah, I had to go to the services on Friday nights as well. That was for about nine or ten months before the actual ceremony. When it was really close, I had classes on my own to learn the portion of the Torah I was going to read.

At our synagogue, everybody stops for refreshments after the Shabbat service. We call this a kiddush. The kiddush is especially big after a Shabbat service when there's a bar mitzvah. This is a time for everybody in the community to celebrate with you. Then, on the same weekend, there's a party as well. Friends and relatives come to the house. We had relatives from America, France, all over Britain, just for me! People always make a big thing of cutting the cake. I had a special fruit cake in the shape of an open book, with lots of icing.

I think most people look forward to their bar mitzvah, because they'll get lots of presents. But often they enjoy it more when they look back on it later, because at the time they're really nervous. I was too busy to get nervous, though.

THINK ABOUT:

Can Jewish children choose whether or not to become bar or bat mitzvah?

What did Ben mean when he said, "I was old enough to know my own mind"?

Why do you think Ben was looking forward to his bar mitzvah?

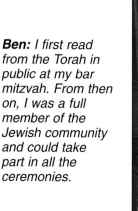

Ben: *I first read from the Torah in public at my bar mitzvah. From then on, I was a full member of the Jewish community and could take part in all the ceremonies.*

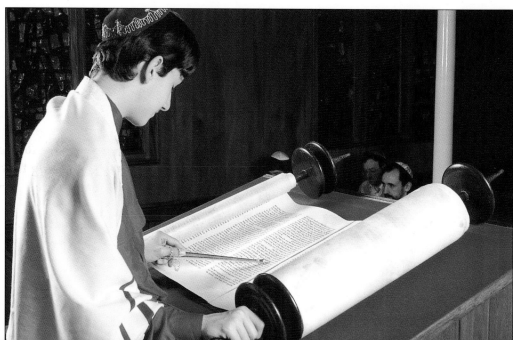

18

Ben: This is my sister Vicky's class, hard at work in Cheder.

I went through my bar mitzvah because I thought that was what everyone did. I didn't question it, but I think I was old enough to know my own mind. Some children at our synagogue do question it, and put it off until they're older. Thirteen is the earliest age anyone can go through their bar mitzvah. For girls it's different. My sister Vicky will be having her **bat mitzvah** when she's twelve.

To a Wonderful Grandson

On his Bar Mitzvah

Ben: When it comes to our bar mitzvah, we have lots of cards from our family and friends.

THINGS TO DO

Design an invitation to a bar or bat mitzvah for people who are not Jewish. You will need to make sure they understand what they are coming to see. Use lettering, pictures or symbols you can find in this book to decorate it.

Imagine you were Ben or Vicky going through their bar or bat mitzvah. What thoughts would have been going through your mind just before you went up to read? Write them down as though you were filling in your diary at the end of the day.

Ben's bar mitzvah was going to affect the rest of his life. Write a story about yourself in which you have to prepare for something that will affect the rest of your life. It is up to you whether or not you write about something that really happened.

Worship in the home

Sarah: *Here is Dad saying kiddush over the wine at our Shabbat meal.*

SARAH We have to say the **Amidah** three times a day. We say it facing Jerusalem. If you can't go to the synagogue, you can say it at home.

We believe we are closest to God when we say the Amidah. So we take three steps backwards and then three steps forward before we say it. We bow as well. It's sort of respectful – like meeting a king.

The most important way we worship at home is by keeping Shabbat. Everything has to be ready by sunset on the Friday night. Mam lights the candles because ladies have to do that. Dad says kiddush (that's a **blessing** over a glass of wine). He says:

> *Blessed are you, Lord our God, King of the Universe,*
> *who creates the fruit of the vine.*
> *Blessed are you, Lord our God, King of the Universe,*
> *who brings forth bread from the earth.*

Then we have the Shabbat meal. It starts with special bread called **challah**.

THINK ABOUT:

In what ways is Shabbat different from the other days of the week? Think about what has been said on pages 10 to 13, as well.

Why is it as important, for a Jew, to worship regularly at home as it is to go to the synagogue?

Why do Jews have so many blessings? Why are some for the most ordinary things in life?

Sarah: *We say prayers from a Siddur. If a Siddur gets ripped or too old to use, you mustn't just throw it away. It has to be buried because God's name's in it. Worn-out Torah scrolls are buried too.*

Sarah: *Shabbat really starts when Mam lights the candles.*

20

At the end of Shabbat we have a short service called **Havdalah**. This is to show that our special day has ended. Dad drinks some wine and lights a special plaited candle. We also have some spices in a special box on the table.

We don't only say blessings on Shabbat. There are blessings for almost everything: when we eat, when we put new clothes on and even when we go to the toilet.

BEN Shabbat is really special; special in a way that is hard to explain if you don't have it. It's a celebration and a way of showing our thanks to the creator of the universe.

Sometimes we say grace after meals on other days of the week. I don't usually say all the blessings. I believe it's what you think that matters not saying things out loud.

Sarah: On the Saturday night, you light a plaited candle. If you don't have one, you can hold two ordinary candles together.

THINGS TO DO

Look for the Havdalah candle, spice box and wine glass in the pictures. Draw them and write a sentence about each one.

What are the things you really feel thankful for in your life? Write them down and say who you would like to thank for them.

Ben says that having Shabbat is very special. Many people don't keep one day separate as a day of rest. What do you think? What would you like about a day like Sarah and Ben's Shabbat? What would you dislike about it? Write what you think in two columns.

Keeping Shabbat

I would enjoy a Shabbat day of rest because:	I would find the Shabbat day of rest difficult because:

Sarah: The smell from the box with spices in it is lovely. It reminds you of the Shabbat feeling all week.

Worship in the synagogue

SARAH When we go to the synagogue, we children sit with Mam and the rest of the women. We don't go for the whole Shabbat service. Mam says it would be too long for Joshua and Malka. We usually arrive just before the reading from the Torah.

We use a Siddur for the service. Most of the service is in Hebrew. That's all right because we learn to read Hebrew in Cheder. There are prayers and blessings. Sometimes the rabbi gives a **sermon** in English.

The part I like best is when they bring the Torah out of the Ark. Some of the men carry it all round the synagogue, before they take it up to the **bimah** to read it. They carry it round again before they put it back. The other men kiss their tallit and touch the scroll with it as it goes past. They do this to show respect because the Torah is so holy.

In the synagogue men and married ladies have to cover their heads. Some of the men wear hats but most use a kippah.

Ben: There are no pictures or statues of God in a synagogue. Instead you will often see beautiful stained glass windows which remind us about our festivals and holidays.

*Sarah: You can see the straps of Rabbi Danny's **tefillin** wound around his left arm.*

Ben: It is a real honour to take the scroll from the Ark. I am allowed to do that since my bar mitzvah.

THINK ABOUT:

Orthodox women sit apart from men during worship and do not take an active part in services. Ben's synagogue is quite different. Even the rabbi is a woman, there. What do you think about these differences?

Why do you think the Jews treat the Torah scrolls with such great respect?

What do you do if you want to show respect to people or special things?

Sarah: No-one is allowed to take pictures in the synagogue on Shabbat but here you can see Rabbi Danny standing where he does for the sermon.

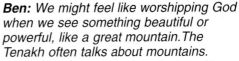

Ben: We might feel like worshipping God when we see something beautiful or powerful, like a great mountain. The Tenakh often talks about mountains.

THINGS TO DO

Look at the pictures in this book that have been taken inside a synagogue. Choose two things that you can see in them that you think are important or interesting. Draw them and say what they are.

Imagine that you have made a long journey to the mountain in the picture. Perhaps it has come into sight for the first time or you have just reached the top of it. Describe what you see and how you feel about it.

Draw two columns on a sheet of paper. Read over this chapter and pages 20 and 21 again. In the first column, make a list of things that Jews do when they worship God. In the second column, write down why they do these things.

Worshipping God	
Things that Jews do	*Why they do them*

FACT FILE

Sermon A talk by a religious leader.

Bimah The platform where the Torah is read in a synagogue.

Tefillin Small boxes with leather straps. There is one for the forehead and one for the left arm. A copy of the Shema is kept in each box. Jews wear them because the Torah tells them to bind the law next to their hearts and minds.

Getting married

Ben: *Here are Mam and Dad cutting their wedding cake.*

BEN I don't know if it would be important to me to marry a Jewish girl. It would depend on the person. In this country, you might meet someone who called themselves a Christian but didn't really follow any religion. If everything else was equal, I think I would prefer someone Jewish.

Dad says our religion is passed down by the mother. A Jewish woman can marry a non-Jew and her children will still be Jewish, but if a Jewish man marries a non-Jewish woman, they won't.

RABBI DANNY A wedding is an important time. The bride and groom make promises to each other. On the day they usually prepare themselves by going without food until the ceremony.

Some people get married in the synagogue but it is quite normal to have the wedding outdoors, under a **chuppah**. The groom and his parents wait there for the bride and her parents to come to them.

There are psalms and special blessings and the couple share two cups of wine. The groom gives the bride a ring which she wears on her right hand during the ceremony.

Ben: *Mam and Dad's ketubah says exactly what they promised each other when they were married.*

corresponding to the 2nd day of November , 1980
the bridegroom *Stanley Jack Soffa*
said to the bride *Diana Frances Cairns*
Be thou my wife according to the Law of MOSES and of ISRAEL. I will cherish and honour and maintain thee in truth and faithfulness as it becometh a Jewish husband to do;
AND the bride assented to the bridegroom's proposal and agreed to be his wife according to the Law of MOSES and ISRAEL, and to cherish and honour her husband as beseemeth a daughter in Israel:
ACCORDINGLY they entered into this holy covenant of love and comradeship, of peace and harmony, to establish a house in Israel to the glory of the Holy and Blessed ONE, who sanctifieth HIS people ISRAEL through the sacred covenant of marriage.
THIS COVENANT was duly executed, signed and witnessed this day.

THINK ABOUT:

If you were choosing a husband or a wife, would it matter to you what religion they were?

Why do you think that it is important for Jews that God is watching over the wedding?

Is it easy to keep promises? What kinds of things help people keep promises?

Ben: *This was the chuppah at Mam and Dad's wedding. You can see the embroidered material. Sometimes the poles at each corner are decorated with flowers.*

The groom has to stamp on a wine glass to break it. Everyone shouts "Mazel Tov". This means "Good Luck". Some people say breaking the glass is to remember our Temple in Jerusalem being destroyed. Others say it reminds the couple that, although everyone quarrels sometimes, they shouldn't let their marriage break like the glass.

At the end of the service the couple sign two marriage papers. One is the same paper that everyone who gets married in Britain has to sign. The other one is special to Jews. It is called the **ketubah**. The ceremony ends, like most weddings, with a big party!

FACT FILE

Chuppah A kind of tent without sides. It stands for the bride and groom's new home.

Ketubah A wedding certificate which includes the duties of both the husband and the wife. It is read out during the service and both sign it to show they agree to the marriage.

THINGS TO DO

Draw a wedding under a chuppah.

Design your own ketubah which sets out what you think people should promise each other when they get married.

Imagine you are the bride or groom at a Jewish wedding.
Describe what happens and what your feelings are.

Celebrating festivals

SARAH We celebrate lots of festivals. Most of them happen at about the same time each year but not on the same date.

I really like festivals. In our family, we always have a great time. Our festivals don't always remember happy things; but there is usually a good story behind them.

Purim was in March this year. It was brilliant! In the synagogue, the children were allowed to wear fancy dress. Someone read the story of Queen Esther from the **megillah** and every time we heard the name **Haman** we went crazy! We had drums and rattles and were shouting and whistling. Some people chalked "Haman" on the bottoms of their shoes and tried to stamp it off. Afterwards, we had great party food. That's because there are lots of feasts in the story. So we remember Esther by eating as much as we can!

Ben: *The beautiful windows around our synagogue remind us of our festivals. This one shows one of the rattles we use to celebrate Purim.*

BEN On the first night of **Pesach**, we have a family meal called a **Seder**. During the meal, we read the story of how God rescued the Jews from slavery in Egypt. At different points in the story, we eat food which reminds us of what our ancestors went through 3,500 years ago. I like the taste of the **charoset** best. It is a reminder of the cement the Jewish slaves had to make; but its sweet taste also reminds us of what it feels like to be free.

Ben: *There is a picture of our family celebrating Pesach on page 4. Here you can see Dad following the Seder in his hagadah.*

THINK ABOUT:

Why do you think children enjoy Purim and Pesach?

What sad things are Jewish people reminded of at Purim?

Why do you think that being free is so important to Jewish people today?